BYTCHE

A COLLECTION OF COMICALLY HORRIFIC FAILED RELATIONSHIPS

BOOK I

BY KEVIN ALLEN

Published by Starry Night Publishing.Com
Rochester, New York

Copyright 2023 Kevin Allen

This book remains the copyrighted property of the author, and may not be reproduced, copied, and distributed for commercial, or noncommercial purposes. Thank you for your support.

Kevin Allen

DEDICATION:

In loving memory of Janet Maxon, my mother. This book was her idea from having listened to my crazy stories over the years. Thank you for pushing me, Mom!

Kevin Allen

Contents

DEDICATION: 3
An introduction to my insanity 7
Chapter 1: The Dog and the Baby. 11
Chapter 2: The Engagement Ring................................. 13
Chapter 3: The Awkward Erection 17
Chapter 4: The Bruce Lee Punch 21
Chapter 5: The Samurai Sword..................................... 25
Chapter 6: The Arsonist.. 29
Chapter 7: The Cutter 31
Chapter 8: The Original Stalker................................... 33
Chapter 9: The Revenge Fornicator............................. 37
Chapter 10: The Misdiagnosis 41
Chapter 11: The Raging Alcoholic 45
Chapter 12: The Martyr and Her Evil Mother 47
Chapter 13: The Bathtub.. 51
Chapter 14: The Convenient Friend............................ 53
Chapter 15: Stockholm Syndrome............................... 55
Chapter 16: The Stripper.. 57
Chapter 17: The Three-Month Marriage 59
Chapter 18: Misery 61
Chapter 19: Narcissist Supreme................................... 65
Sum it all up:.. 69

Kevin Allen

<u>An introduction to my insanity:</u> The Girl at Social Security and the Girl on the bus. The Same Old Situation.

The title of the book is very misleading, as I don't really feel that way. I don't think at all that ALL the women I dated were crazy, and I don't approve of referring to women as bytches. In fact, it is quite to the contrary. I believe that I am a common denominator in all this, and most likely, the crazy one. I mean, do the math. There are about 20 relationships where things went terribly wrong, and I chose all of them, yep me. There will be two more editions to this book, and the second edition, is from the perspective of the women I dated, if, of course, if I am able to interview them. There are always two sides to every story. I am just as responsible as they are, perhaps even more. Even though there are no names used in this book, it's only fair to give them a voice as well.

There are probably reasons why I made these decisions which I will go into very briefly and not elaborate on at length. When I was young, I was a very troublesome child. I could blame people, but, in the end, the choices were mine. All of this led to me eventually getting sent to a foster home. My family believed that this was the only way to help me. They eventually did choose to take me back, and our relationship is beautiful, however, the damage is done. I believe that this somehow led me to unconsciously choose relationships that were doomed to fail.

One of the very few, that I let my guard down for, and opened my heart up too, died of an epileptic seizure very suddenly. It seems that even when I chose the right one, it was still doomed.

That being said, this prelude is designed to illiterate that fact, and provide some insight to how much I actually attract craziness. It is not done on a conscious level at all. These upcoming examples will hopefully draw a picture of how crazy just loves to cling to me like a magnet on the refrigerator.

The title of this book was created purely for marketing purposes. whether you think it's silly, or I pissed you off oh, you picked it up didn't you.

The first example I will use is the girl on the bus. I was fleeing what was undoubtedly the WORST relationship I've ever had. This relationship will be discussed in a later chapter, named misery, yeah, after the movie. the one where she hobbled the guy breaking his freaking leg.

I was on a bus traveling across the country to put some distance between myself and a monster, I mean girlfriend I had. I had literally just gotten away from some intense insanity, just to let it find me again, if only briefly. Uh, no thanks! As soon as I sat down on the bus, I noticed this girl staring me down. I didn't see it so much; however, I could feel it on the back of my neck like the sun, being focused through a magnifying glass, on an ant. The evil was upon me yet again. I wanted nothing to do with whatever fresh hell this was, or any situation after what I just went through. I just wanted to get the f*** away.

After about 20 minutes or so of feeling a flu level nauseous uneasiness, I randomly checked the surrounding area hoping not to be noticed, to see what horror was plotting to pray on me. I took a chance and looked back and accidentally made eye contact with it. Nooooooooooooooooooooooooooo!!!!!! What have I done? I just invited the vampire into my house!!! AHHHHHHHHH!!!

Within seconds she made her way over to me and sat down next to me. After introducing herself she promptly asked me if I had any Adderall. Yep, here we go again. I assured her I did not. She got borderline aggressive about asking me if I was sure. I finally convinced her I did not have any. I do actually have ADHD, however, I do not take the meds that would normally be prescribed, as I feel they are toxic.

The rest of the trip was her telling me horror stories where apparently, she was the monster, and a very scary one at that. I'm talking fangs, people! The one that stayed in my head is the one where she openly admitted to stabbing her boyfriend in the lower back and watching what she thought was his liver coming out. What in the crazy ass, Twilight Zone, freaking horror movie did I just land in. WOW, just wow. If there is crazy within a 20-mile radius, it's going to find me. JUST LOVELY!!!!!

The other instance I am using to hopefully help my readers understand my dilemma is about a girl I met at the Social Security office. I had gone to the Social Security office to get a new social security card oh, so that I may have a passport.

I was with my father and quite ironically was trying to explain how crazy has a habit of choosing me. It was obvious that he thought I was full of s***. He was about to be proven very wrong.

Just like on the bus there was another creature of the night sitting there, silently watching, waiting to pounce. I told Pops to look over in the upper left corner chair and be careful not to get noticed and that she was sizing me up to somehow, "SAVE HER," OH JOY!

My father without saying a word gave me a look that said b*******. Oh yeah, I said, watch this. I didn't want to do this but my father had to understand. I looked over and smiled and sure enough, she made her way over to us and released her little version of hell. My dad was dumbfounded. She was the victim in her story, nobody was helping her, nothing was fair, everyone else was at fault. She didn't straight up ask, but it was obvious what she was after. I don't really need to say any more about this one, as we got called up soon after, and we got the HELL out of there before she was able to sink her teeth in.

Well, that's it for my prelude. I hope it sets the stage for the wackiness that follows.

Kevin Allen

Chapter 1: The Dog and the Baby.

    This situation was nutty enough just concerning the dog however when I tell you about the baby situation at the end it becomes unbelievably nutty. The decision to form a relationship was made entirely too fast, as has been the problem in the past many times.

    The relationship started right away with a big red flag. When I say big red flag, I mean TITANIC sized, big ole red flag waving majestically in my face, for me to overlook, like a poop throwing monkey. I wonder why this crap keeps happening to me, LOL? Oh, shut up, that was a rhetorical question. She lived in one city and I lived in another. We decided to rent a hotel room halfway and go out for a little bit and have some fun. She asked if she could bring her dog. As a fellow dog lover, I did not protest. That doesn't seem like a red flag, right? Well, it didn't to me either. Boy was I ever f****** wrong. It wasn't until we were sharing a moment of intimacy, that I should have realized I was in trouble and ran. Yeah, yeah, everyone reading this knows precisely why I didn't run. Blah, blah, blah. While we are in the middle of intercourse, her dog was running circles around the bed howling like a rabid werewolf. This was definitely a WTF moment, and a big one. She dismissed it like it wasn't even happening, like it was a normal occurrence. I'm not sure how I was able to pretend like I wasn't experiencing holocaust level horror, but I did. O.K., O.K., the sex was really good, ya happy? My dumb ass stayed with her, making weird excuses for it in my head, probably because of it. I'm an idiot. This is where I need to take accountability for being a very large part of the problem. I could have walked away here, but EVIDENTALLY, I just love torturing myself.

    I thought the situation was manageable but it was not. After a while the dog situation got more and more ridiculous. I understand loving her dog, I still cry when I think about my dog I lost. I bet you're wondering how it became unmanageable. Lucky for you, I'm going to tell you!

Kevin Allen

She slept downstairs on a mattress and not up in her bedroom so her very old dog could sleep with her. I get it the dog was Old, she was being sweet. When does sweet turn into disgusting, borderline bestiality behavior you wonder? All right, here goes. Her dog insisted on sleeping with her ass right in her face. Not a big deal you say? Did I mention the dog had absolutely no control over its fucking bowel movements? There were about ten different sheets overlapping one another so that when the dog would shit mid sleep, she could just take one off. I even suggested putting a doggie bed right next to her bed, you know, to avoid feces. Crazy, what was I thinking? She would wake up every night to a giant pit-bull size turd spiraling towards her forehead, like a stinky torpedo from an enemy butthole! As a bonus, sometimes it even made it to her forehead. I'm not sure if I can think of anything that turns me off as much as dogshit in between my girlfriend's eyes! Yep! you read that right, no I'm serious, fecal matter to the face!

This person lacks the ability to find the understanding why I no longer wished to be intimate with her. Let me break it down for you.

Not now, not ever, in this lifetime or the next, will I EVER, have sex with anyone who allows their pet to DEFICATE IN THEIR FACE!!!!!! I still can't understand why she had a hard time grasping that situation. I draw the line at feces. Let's just keep our intercourse and cuddling time poop free, shall we? Also, EWWWWWWWWWW

But wait, there's more. if that wasn't enough, she contacted me a month after we broke up and asked if I was still going to provide her with a baby. A BABY? WHAT? HUH? Did I hear that right? Did the girl that enabled her dog to a level that it was okay for it the s*** in her face really just ask me if I was still going to give her a baby? When the fuck was that on the table. The answer is no I'm not giving you a baby, as a matter of fact, you should probably not have kids at all! If you do, good luck raising those future criminals!

I did a little digging oh, and discovered that I was always just a vehicle to her for my genetics. Flattering, yes, weird/ oh absolutely. Terrifying? Yeah that!

Chapter 2: The Engagement Ring

    This person I decided to spend my time with was the most insane person I've ever met and I've met a lot of crazy people. When I say crazy, I mean she was having sex with Saltines. She is fucking crackers! This does not make her a bad person and she was very sweet; she was just insane. We bonded because we both had a loved one who passed away not too long before we met. I tried to remain friends with her as she was essentially a good person but her craziness was just too much. I actually witnessed her getting Baker acted. For those of you that require explanation, that's when they show up, and take someone away.

    I was a bartender by trade, and every time I would get a job she would come in and ruin it for me, by behaving in the most obnoxious, pee on my lawn, asinine fashion!!! I remember one time a group of very well tipping, female customers asked me for a check, mainly because they didn't buy tickets for the circus of madness that was unfolding in front of them. I had a feeling it was because of her. I discreetly winked at them and said hold on just a minute. I gave them what they thought was their check but it had writing on it. It said don't worry you can stay, she's leaving shortly oh, and she's not coming back. This would have been the third job if she ruined it for me. So, the owner took pity on me and banned her from the establishment. She still managed to get food from the drive through and delight us all with her patented form of very loud crazy, by yelling out private information through said drive through window. At this point it changed from horrifying to pure entertainment. "Everyone be quiet for a minute, she's about to be at the window, let's guess what ridiculous shit is going to come out of her mouth today!!!!" I kind of started to feel bad for her, but my bar guests began looking forward to the reality TV show that was transpiring in front of them EVERY TIME I WORKED!!!!

    She actually even tried to be somewhat of a sugar Mommy to me, which I abhorred, once I realized what she was doing. She did not want me to have a job. She wanted me to be her man toy/caretaker. OH GREAT, JUST LOVELY. I remember when I was little thinking, oh yeah, this is what I want to be. Um yeah, NO!!!

I met her in Virginia while I was bartending at a very snooty bar that catered to the local politicians. I'll never forget how the entire country was in a recession, yet the politicians' backyard was doing better than ever. This tells me all I need to know about politicians. I eventually moved back to Florida, and blow and behold, she followed me soon after. It was just a coincidence she was in the same city in the same town less than 5 miles away from me, she insisted. Gee, how could it be anything else. How silly of me to assume. A little insight for those of you who are not as familiar with crazy as I am. They are almost always smart, and know how to manipulate the people around them into believing what they want them to. This person actually had my own friends believing that this VERY close proximity move was a mere coincidence. YEAH RIGHT. The only way to deal with it was to let her prove my point for me given time.

I told you I witnessed her getting Baker acted, and it wasn't just once. When I was in Florida I stayed with a friend for a little while so I can look for a place to stay. She decided to buy two rabbits for me, while I was staying at a friend's house. First of all, I do not want the responsibility. second of all was not my house and my friend did not want pets. Third of all, WTF? Who even does that? I mean, it was a sweet gesture, but I'm staying with a friend. Her thought process does not compute! She did name them Marvel and DC, which besides myself I have to admit that was pretty cool.

Okay, enough of the introduction to the mayor of Wacky Town. This chapter is supposed to be about an engagement ring see, if you haven't gathered that from the title.

So, I went to relax at a cigar bar that I frequent where I knew the owner. I stopped at a few places along the way. Everywhere I went people kept saying congratulations. I thought this was just an elaborate ruse my friends had perpetrated, so I brushed it off with a slight sense of confusion, not knowing the insanity that waited, lurking in the shadows, waiting for the right moment to attack.

I kept asking for what I was being congratulated for, and the response was always a hug, some weird giddiness, and sometimes even a little laughter.

I was so confused. I finally pulled the owner of the cigar bar aside and asked if they're playing a prank on me or something. How did one of my friends manage to get so many people involved? She said no honey, your friend stopped by today and showed everyone the lovely engagement ring that you bought her, and she stated that she didn't even know we were together. Wow, that's funny, cuz NEITHER THE FUCK DID I!!! I thought I was off the crazy train, but alas, I was not. That train for me was like The Hotel California.

I think this ends the engagement ring part of this here.

I would like to end on 1 disgusting point. This is just to paint, again, a lovely brown picture. Why am I consistently ending up with a s*** end of the stick, quite literally!

One time I was supposed to meet her at her hotel room, as she had begged me over and over and over and over to meet with her. I agreed to go eat some chicken wings with her or something like that. She was not answering her phone and when I got there, and her hotel room door was ajar. I was terrified to enter it as she drank a lot and feared the worst. Well, it wasn't the worst thing, but it was still pretty crappy.

She was laying naked in her bed, with her clothes all over the room with her bottom covered in, you guessed it, FECES. What a treat!!! And here I thought she didn't get me anything. Yep, like a freaking toddler. I very quietly turned around, locked the door, closed it ever so gently, and got the FUCK out of there. I think I am done dealing with feces as the last two chapters have somehow been focused on it Hooray for me!!! I think I'm done writing for the night; I'm pooped.

Kevin Allen

Chapter 3: The Awkward Erection

    This one was very short-lived. It started out as fun, however it quickly turned into a nightmare.

    I was working at this very popular tourist trap in Florida. This very cute little blond thing asked me where the bathroom was. Being a die-hard Ace Ventura fan, I immediately asked, "number one or number two," followed by, "I just want to know how much time I have." She laughed very charitably, and awkwardly continued her journey to the restroom.

    When she emerged, she promptly invited me out for a drink or two, or 15. All I can remember from the whole night is doing shots of 151 rum at her beach apartment. One thing led to another; you can figure it out.

    In the morning she acted very strange, so I reluctantly left my number, took hers and exited. It was an awkward situation. I'm guessing that she was still drunk and had holes in her memory about the night.

    I gave her a few days and called her and she decided to meet me out a few days later. When I arrived at the designated place, she eventually admitted that when she woke up, she didn't know who I was and was very happy it was me, the guy from the restaurant. I of course ignored the right red flag that she had just set on fire in front of me. Nope, didn't even notice the big red flag right in my stupid face! Why should I learn from all the other bright red flags? Why should I wander back onto the pages of this lovely young woman's horror novel?

    For a short time, fun ensued, it was actually nice…

    Okay, the fun part was very short-lived, now to the crazy stuff. She invited me to her apartment again, but I don't think she realized she had invited me to a different apartment than the last time. I didn't say anything but she didn't seem like she could afford 2 apartments. We end up having some drinks, things happen. The morning comes, and things are happening again. The reason I am making you aware of the things is, because it's PARAMOUNT to the rest of the story.

All of a sudden, she is all flustered, and starts begging me to hide in the closet as, "He," is here. HOW DELIGHTFUL!!!

I say, absolutely not, I had no idea you were involved with someone else, and I'm a grown man. I am not hiding in the closet. This is your problem now you have to deal with it, frankly I'm disgusted.

She finally convinces me to hide in the closet still naked, I should add. This is when I make a horrible observation, I still have an erection. Did I tell you I still had an erection, because I still had an erection. an awkward erection if you will. Yep, a lingering stiffy, a persistent boner, was I experiencing a priapism, this is my life right now???!!! This timing is just soooooo wrong.

This man opens a closet door, all the time yelling at her looking for something. He is so enamored with looking for something, that he does not notice the naked man, with an erection still, I should add, sitting on the floor, like ET amongst the stuffed animals in that closet. Was I invisible? I mean, I am literally sitting on the floor, yes, somehow still with, you guessed it, an erection that for some reason will NOT go away. Was this the elusive fear boner I've always heard about? I thought that was just a myth. Oh my God the fear boner is real. AHHHHHHHHH!!! I think I'll go hunting unicorns later. I eventually come to the conclusion that the way I am sitting is pinching something somehow and making it so the blood stays in the one place I do not want it.

He started berating her for taking all the Xanax he had left for her. I'm guessing she needed it to be able to do the things, and the stuff with this awful man. Oh boy, here we go! A nasty argument ensues. I decide to stay there, and avoid the situation at all costs, until I hear her hit the wall, bounce off said wall and then hit the floor. She let out a cry for help.

At this point I had no other choice but to come out. This is where my idiot friends just love to make, coming out of the closet jokes. LOLOLOLOLOLOLOLOLOL Did I mention I still had an erection, cuz I still have an erection!!! This all happened very quickly and I sincerely hope, it would have diminished if I had more time. Was I kneeling in a position that somehow restricted blood flow, like I thought? I mean it really was not a priapism or anything. Lord help me! Great timing!!!

Bytches Be Crazy

Upon exiting the closet, mind you still naked, still with an erection, I say, look dude, I don't care what this is, or who you are, nor do I want anything to do with either of you. I am not, however, going to let you hurt her. So, unless you want to get your ass kicked by a naked man, I suggest you don't put your hands on her. He was terrified. I mean, picture it. On second thought, no, please do not.

He then tries to explain how it is her fault, and how she's a whore, and how I shouldn't trust her. I explained to him that I want nothing to do with her or him. I am simply getting her out of the house and away from him. I asked him not to speak with me before I snap and just let me get my damn pants on and get the fuck away from those two crazy people. I never wanted to see either of them, ever again.

I took her to what she said was her mother's house and dropped her off. At least she was safe. I was disgusted with the whole situation. I felt a great deal of relief, as I thought it was over.

You thought it was over too, didn't you? Guess what, of course it wasn't. She shows up at my job with some guy with her arm around him, in an attempt to make me jealous. She walked over to the stairs, and looked back to see if I'm getting jealous. As she sticks her tongue out at me, engaging in some kind of weird high school display of immaturity, she actually falls up the stairs, almost taking him with her. Everyone within eye shot at the restaurant, once they realize she was okay, of course, just about died with hysterical laughter

Okay now it's over

Kevin Allen

Chapter 4: **The Bruce Lee Punch**

This person definitely was not crazy, just hurting and upset. The situation was however crazy, which warrants its presence in this book.

This was my first real relationship, and it was with a very caring, gentle, thoughtful human being. I can't stress that part enough. I kicked myself, and often still do for walking away from this one.

Of course, it didn't work out, which seems to be the norm for me. If I was reading this, I would immediately make the observation that I very well might be the problem. I am aware of the redundancy on many levels here.

At first, she wouldn't have me, even though we cuddled every night together, as she felt she should remain loyal to her current boyfriend who I knew wasn't right for her. She just didn't want to hurt him. Funny thing, this was college, and somehow that was acceptable. It's not.

We all had left for college for the summer. I had made her promise that when she returned, if she had chosen me, instead of her current boyfriend, to wear this specific sweatshirt I bought her. I was certain it would be me.

She showed up wearing the sweatshirt. I was so excited; I was running through the dorm to meet her. Yes, I was totally staring out the window, waiting for her to return. I couldn't eat or sleep, until I knew. I was devastated when she explained to me that it was not me she had chosen. Why would she be so cruel to wear the sweatshirt, just to play with my emotions. It was not her intention to hurt me like that. Her idea was to let me know that she loved me, even if I wasn't the one she chose. It really sucked. I was so distraught that I vowed to make her fall for me and crush her. This was the beginning of my obsession with working out. It began with revenge. The code for this horrible idea, between my roommate and I, was Game Plan. I am aware that this is very immature, but I was heartbroken, and I was 18.

Kevin Allen

On Valentine's Day, the guy was coming to visit her, and I requested that she at least see us in the same room together before she let me go, completely. She did just that, and realized her true feelings were for me. I really felt sorry for the guy. I saw him walking home alone from the party that we all went to, and picked him up and gave him a ride. He really handled it well. He was a nice guy. I knew she was going to choose me all along, even though I had been wrong before.

I realized the plan to hurt her was immature, foolish, and Immediately abandoned it. I could never go through with it anyway.

Eventually the relationship failed mostly due to us, being young and not ready, but mostly due to my immaturity.

After some time passed, I made a friend with a female I was attracted to. We were just friends at the moment. All of the sudden my ex wants to be best friends with her. Little did I know that this was the recipe for about 75% of the situations I was to experience in the future.

The new person and I were watching a movie together rather innocently I might add, when the ex showed up. I was upset as this was not a coincidence and in bad form.

I proceeded to inform my ex as to how poor and desperate her behavior was. I'll admit I was very insensitive, no, I was an asshole. She reacted by using a technique I showed her to defend herself. She executed it perfectly and broke my nose. She went to swing at me again and I responded by subduing her, without hurting her I might add, or causing her any pain. I was just trying to avoid getting punched in the nose again, or her hurting herself. She began yelling at me, for defending myself. I can imagine that in her eyes it may have appeared aggressive. I grabbed my nose and moved it back and forth showing her that it undoubtedly had been broken.

She started crying and apologizing profusely. My anger for her actions subsided immediately because I was impressed how she executed that move better than I ever could. I was also very concerned for her, because that behavior was far out of the realm of her character. She was and still is one of the best people I have ever met.

As for the aftermath, she was instructed by the college to seek counseling or be expelled. She chose counseling, thank God.

I was the resident assistant on my dorm room floor. I was given the option of performing all the RA Duties, or be removed from the dorms. I did not think that was fair, as I felt innocent in all that transpired.

I decided to move off campus with some old friends from high school that happened to go to the same college.

Yep, you guessed it, her new best friend was one of my roommates. I did not approve of course. This ridiculous behavior proved to be the case, in most of my future relationship endeavors. Everyone told me not to be so conceited, that it wasn't always about me. Okay, maybe it wasn't. Maybe she needed someone to cuddle with. Maybe it makes her happy. I will say one thing though. The women who have done this, as some strange attempt to get at me, or whatever they're trying to do, just ends up hurting the people they use to do it, and it is inexcusable. This ends up happening to several of my friends in the future. I blame myself somewhat.

The best part of this situation is that she had to actually walk through my room to leave or enter his, so I was forced to see her often. HOW CONVENIENT. Odd, that she would choose tha K9t roommate. How conceited of me to assume it was about me. It's not like I was 100% correct or anything. I should add that on her part it was most likely done on an unconscious level. One morning when she walked through my room, she found me with somebody else. I did not know she was there at the time, or I wouldn't have done it. Also, I drank A tremendous amount of beer in college. She freaked out and walked for about 10 miles in the snow, or so I was told, and had to be picked up by friends. This was just the beginning of my insane experiences, and is was very mild compared to the rest so keep reading my friends. If this was done in chronological order this would have been first, but there is no order, only chaos, buwahahahahahah!!!

There is a moral to this story. do not teach your significant other martial arts unless you plan on remaining with them forever.

Kevin Allen

Chapter 5: The Samurai Sword

This one is a doozy. I was living with the super cute girl I had been dating in a pay per week apt/hotel at the beach. How do we end up there? Well, that's a story for another time. I got home from work a little late, and gently nudged her, so I can have a spot on the bed to sleep, as I just worked a double shift, absolutely exhausted.

She decided to respond by grabbing my index finger and middle finger, bending them back in an attempt to break them. This is when I should have walked away for good, by my dumb ass of course did not. WTF DUDE!!!! I assumed she was in the middle of a bad dream and gave her the benefit of the doubt.

I did however decide that it may be better for me to sleep on the couch in the other room as it was a much better/safer place.

After some time passed, she inquired as to whether or not I was coming to bed, not acknowledging her sit decision earlier to try and break my damn fingers. I mean why not just pretend it didn't happen.

I calmly said, I'd be there shortly but needed to watch the news to see if the weather was going to affect work for the following day. That was a lie, fabricated by me to give her time to calm down, and to avoid any more conflict.

My memory of the rest of the night is clouded as I was half asleep, but I do remember her chasing around the apartment with my samurai sword, or Katana if you will.

Things got pretty rough; she pretty much beat the s*** out of me. If you're wondering, no there was not a scratch on her, because I didn't touch her. You couldn't even see the whites in one of my eyeballs because of all the blood in it.

I decided it best to stay somewhere else after finally getting away from her. I realized I had her car keys and that she had to work the next day, so I was going to very quietly return them to her, and get the fuck out of there! Why was it so difficult to get past her to get my wallet in my pants, you asked? It presented a problem because she was standing in front of them with one of my FRIGGIN SAMURAI SWORDS. I wasn't exactly going to leave in my Underpants, as that would have presented its own set of problems. This is why I did not just leave. After I left, I realized I had the keys to her car somehow and decided to return them oh, hopefully without getting noticed. I knew she had to work that next day.

Upon my return, the police were there. They were pretty civil, until the sheriff left and put his Deputy in charge. The deputy immediately decided that I was guilty mainly because I had a male genitalia. He proceeded to try to bully me into a fight, so he can taze me and or beat the shit out of me. To avoid that situation from happening, I got on my hands and knees, taking the most passive position I could possibly think of. I asked the deputy very humbly to look at my face carefully so that he could notice all the blood and bruises on me and then compare the lack thereof on her face. There was not a mark on her. Nothing at all. He even asked me why I didn't just leave if I meant no harm. Well officer, I was in my underwear, and she was guarding my pants, and my wallet with a friggin' sword, so I could not leave. I'm guessing you would have arrested me for walking down the road in my skivvies, would you not?

The deputy, much to my bewilderment, and disbelief decides not to take just her, but both of us to jail. Why on Earth was he taking me to jail? Was it simply because I had a phallus? When I arrived in jail, the cop looked at me in the light, and said, wow, she really did a number on you. WTF? Was that his way of saying sorry I took you to jail? Again, why was I even there? He should have taken me home, ASSHOLE! FYI, I have an affection for the police, as my Grandpa was one of the very first Italians to be given that honor years ago in NY State.

While in jail for the weekend, I was often asked why I was there. I told them because I got my ass kicked by a little tiny girl. At the time I was about 250 lbs., mostly muscle. I guess I could see where they would think that I was full of it, but I really didn't think it was fair either.

Eventually we went to go see a judge on a little circuit TV in a small room where a bunch of the trustees and guards were there as well. A lot of the trustees were also the ones that did not believe me. Boy were they in for it! Never did I ever think I would get excited about proving that I got my ass kicked by a tiny little girl to a bunch of trustees in jail, yet, there I was. HOLY SHIT!!!

My girlfriend, also known as the guilty party, tried to address the judge, begging for release on her own recognizance, or ROR, if you will. She stated that she had a job she didn't want to lose, had no priors, and was a good person.

The judge very sternly said he did not want to talk to her and you would rather speak to me. He asked if I thought she should be released on ROR, if she would try to hurt me again, if she would hurt herself, or anyone else. I very quietly said, yes judge, you should let her go. The judge said speak up or I'm not inclined to believe you. Like an idiot I did speak up and got her out. I still wonder if I should have just let her stay there. I know I'm an idiot.

When I returned to jail, I was greeted with hysterical laughter. The trustees said things like, wow, your big ass did get kicked by a little girl. Ha-ha, very funny guys, I retorted. Strangely, it made me some friends.

I allowed her to remain in my life, in that little apartment. She had no place else to go, or so I thought. She started acting up again, following having several drinks. I asked her if she had a family that would help her, if she wasn't without a place to stay. She assured me her family would never leave her out to dry.

I replied with a big fat, GET THE FUCK OUT! I should have done that a long time ago. Jeez, that feels good just writing it. My palms are sweaty!

I should also add that while I was in jail, they wanted to treat me for head trauma. Yeah, you heard that right, head trauma. I had to have had some head trauma to let that girl stay in my life. Also, I no longer have swords.

Kevin Allen

Chapter 6: The Arsonist

This chapter has a very short one, as was… … whatever her and I shared. It was not a relationship by conventional means, just two people having fun, with alcohol involved.

I had been visiting this person every now and then, and we always had a lot of fun together, however, I sensed something was amiss. GO FIGURE, what a surprise!

One night I showed up and she was just sitting there in the dark staring at the candles she had carefully placed around the entire circumference of the room. She was staring at the candles so attentively I could barely get her attention. This was odd because usually when I visited, she was all about us having fun.

I knew I was going to regret this next question, but I asked anyway. I asked her if there was something I should know, and why was she so enamored with the candles, more specifically, the fire on top of the candles.

Let's just say her answer, not only surprised me, but terrified me. She said, well I just got out of prison for arson. Oh boy, we got a live one here. Her just getting out of prison explained a few things, but I'm not going to elaborate, because that is not what this book is about. You did it again, buddy ole pal, you picked a winner.

My response was to wet my fingertips and proceeded to put out all the candles as quickly as I could. Tsss, tsss, tsss, was all that was heard for the next minute or two. Tsss

I then apologized, and took my leave. Given my experience, had I stayed, it would have eventually ended very badly. I don't think I could pull off the Freddy Krueger look.

Chapter 7: The Cutter

This one is especially unfortunate because this person was funny, intelligent, fun to be around, and an overall good person. She was just as aware she was crazy as I am. She tried to take measures to thwart it, but there were too many other variables in the way.

Like every short story in this book, I was one of those variables. Sometimes I walked away for my own sanity, and other times it was for the other parties' benefit, but in this case, it was better for the both of us.

She had been infatuated with me as a kid, probably because out of the group of my idiot friends, I was definitely the nice one. I may have even been the only nice one. O.K. there was one other nice one.

As fate will have it over 20 years, after our childhood friendship, social media did its thing and brought us together. I was intrigued by the fact that she was a writer that likes to drink. Back then I very much liked to drink. I know what you're thinking, and you're right! .PART OF THE PROBLEM!!!! Wow, you sure are perceptive.

Over and over, if she couldn't get me to behave in the manner in which she wanted, she would become visibly upset, even if she tried her best to hide it, because she wasn't doing it on purpose, and she knew it was driving us apart. Her attempts at hiding her displeasure were very unsuccessful.

Eventually that behavior was obviously unhealthy for her, and my behavior was just throwing gas on that fire. Again, none of this was done purposely by either party.

I did the math, and came up with the calculation that I was not healthy for her, and should stay away.

This is where it gets a little crazy. If I sound like I am painting her in a negative image, it is not my intention, but I'm telling the story.

Her response was to send me a picture of a plastic shaving razor, like the one you would use on your legs or your face. She then sent me a second picture of said razor deconstructed, all its parts carefully weighed out and a very OCD manor. The third picture was the most disturbing. She had sent me pictures of cut marks all over her arms. It looked like she had just gotten in a fight with a blood lusted Wolverine and lost. I wasn't aware that they made those razors with adamantium.

This was not only dangerous, and severely unhealthy for her, it was also one of the most selfish things I can imagine. She was playing on my compassion to get me to come over although I did not wish to.

This is by definition a sickness. I would even guess a bit sociopathic, however, I do not have the proper education to diagnose such a thing.

I ended it by contacting a relative of hers to make sure she was safe, and then blocking her on all forms of media.

You think this was the end of it wouldn't you. nope my dumbass decided it wasn't. Big emphasis on the dumbass part. We somehow got back in contact over five years later. She told me that she was taking meds so that she could maintain a normal life. I decided to give it another go around. I learned two very valuable lessons. The first being, if it doesn't work the first time, it's not going to work the second time. The second lesson was that medication does not work if you drink like a fish on it. In fact, it would be quite the opposite and compound exponentially whatever problems exist to begin with, and most likely add a few more.

When I say drink, I mean nearly a whole box of wine. How many glasses are in a box of wine, you say? 15 to 20, depending on the size! Holy shit, wow, I'm lucky to be alive. Okay, that part was a joke, she was a good person, and I never felt like I was in danger. Sometimes people have a lot of bad things happen to them and don't respond very well. I should know as I am one of them

Chapter 8: **The Original Stalker**

Things began with this one innocently enough. I was working on the beach at a party restaurant, and we all stayed after to drink, as we usually did. I can't remember a night where the servers didn't stay and get drunk a bunch of tourists.

I had a bit too much to drink, as was the norm, and this nice, really pretty waitress offered to give me a ride home.

We sat in the driveway and talked for a while outside of my house and ended up kissing. I decided to stop, because of the work rule, you know, don't s*** where you eat! She stated that she was going back to college in a few months. As far as I was concerned this was a loophole in that rule, so I caved. This marked the beginning of several nutty mc nut bar situations.

Jumping more towards the end of this, I became concerned about a possible age difference. Specifically, because she had this unbearably annoying habit of adding an a at the end of words or phrases. Stop it-a, No-a, Oh my God-a People my age don't talk like that. I became a bit concerned. Actually, I was more than a bit concerned. SHIT!!! Oh boy, this is going to be a problem.

The really really fun part was I made this observation during a short vacation we went on.

I needed to know what her real age was. I had seen her go into bars several times and not get carded, so why would I not think she wasn't older than she professed.

I came up with a brilliant idea, or at least I thought. It has been my observation that any time someone shows you their driver's license picture and says look how bad this horrible picture is, the other person says, nope, mine is worse, and immediately shows you theirs. This is how I decided I was going to figure out how old she was. I employed the idea. She showed me her ID. My plan was foolproof!!!! I felt so very clever. Who was a big boy? I was a big boy!!! Her ID showed that she was 27 years old. I was soooooo relieved. What a weight lifted off me. I felt so calm. WAIT, aw crap!!!!!!!!!!!, I noticed something else right before she put the ID away. I noticed that the last name on the ID was not the same as the last name she had told me. BINGO!!!! YAHTZEE, DING DING DING, what'll ya have for him Johnny. Prize shown, AN ABSOLUTE NIGHTMARE!!!

The age difference was too much for me, but it wasn't like she was a minor or anything. She was 20, and I was 29. I was too much for me at that age, and it was really upsetting that she was dishonest about it.

I ended the relationship shortly after, but not before quite the entourage of craziness. She stalked me relentlessly!! She had an armoire filled with stuff that I had set down, like empty beer cups, and who knows what else. I know this because now we are friends and we still laugh about it at times.

I discovered that she used to follow me to whatever bar I was at and give people money to buy me shots so it'd be more easily manipulated. I have to admit my part in this, and say that often it worked. Crazy attracts crazy after all.

Some good did come out of a crazy stalking. One time my car broke down and she just happened to be driving by. How strange that she was two car lengths behind me, AGAIN. I complained, but she did pull over and help me out. May I remind you that this book is about crazy situations, sometimes even bad situations, but most of the stories in here are about good people. There are a few bad ones, who will be more towards the end of this book, as it gave me PTSD to even think about writing about them, so I saved them for last. Everybody is either capable of, or has done crazy things in their life. Most people, in fact, have. I certainly have done my share. It just seemed that I have been in the center of it all more often than not.

On a silly note, she would call me from a local bar saying her car died every now and then, begging me to come get her. I would drive there to help her out. Even though she drove me nuts it didn't make her a bad person. I would NEVER let her be stranded. She knew this, and used it. I would show up, open the hood of a car, put the battery cable back on and start it. No, I did not let her drive, I'm not cruel. to be honest this genius technique ended up working a few times. I'm just as guilty as her. Maybe she would have stopped stalking me if I had stopped enabling it.

Bytches Be Crazy

On one occasion I came home to her naked, drunk, rolling around in my bed, having crawled through my window. One time I even had somebody with me. If you haven't figured it out, that person turned around and left immediately. Whatever, it's not like I can entertain a guest and take care of a drunk friend at the same time. Wow. I find myself saying wow a lot.

After all was said and done this one has a good ending. I ended up with a friend, and a pretty good one. So much so at one point I had a date with me at the beach and saw she was bartending at a very popular bar as she was very pretty and a very good bartender. I explained to my date that that was the girl I had spoken about. My date was like, no s*** really, I have got to meet her. What the hell? Why not? I brought my date up to the bar to meet her, and before I could say anything my old stalker/friend said, with a smile, Hi, I'm his original stalker.

She and I have been friends ever since. She was just young, but definitely some craziness happened. No harm done oh, just really crazy stories!!!

Kevin Allen

Chapter 9: **The Revenge Fornicator**

This one almost made me feel bad writing about it, but it's just too nuts not to. Please remember, I am writing about the craziness, and that doesn't mean this person didn't have a slew of good qualities. Before I type another word, I want to make two things clear.

1. This person is still my friend.

2. She is a very good person

I broke up with her for quite a few reasons. I guess walking away was permission for her to make me jealous using people I know. I'm including people I work with, but first let's describe the main reason I left, the massive enabling of her son. I'll demonstrate this with one example.

Against my adamant disagreement, due to a promise of no trouble, I got her son a job where I was working. Let's just get right to it shall we.

Her son got caught selling drugs the very first day within just a few hours.

Her response was, but everyone does drugs, so what's the big deal? Oh, I don't know, because it's my f****** job and the fact that I had to lay it on the line to keep him out of jail, and I even found a way to save his job!

Funny, his response was very similar. He actually said, Well I didn't know I wasn't supposed to. You didn't know you weren't supposed to sell drugs at the job your mother's boyfriend gave you? WOW! WOW! WOW! Are you f****** kidding me. Well golly gee buddy in that case no harm done. f****** idiot! as a matter of fact my very large friend looked at him dead in the face after hearing him say that, and said hey kid don't take a s*** on table 21. You getting the metaphor here? UNBELIEVABLE!!!!!

Sticking my neck out for him was at the cost of losing favor with my boss, and this is what I got 3 days later.

She says, my son is really mad at you cuz you told everyone at work he was selling drugs. Are you f****** kidding me, everyone f****** told me. I saved his f****** job you f****** a******!

This was the beginning of the end of our relationship without a doubt. This kid drove around in his mommy's car with his bong and his video game console at all times, and he was enabled to the point that he didn't know what right or wrong was.

Another time he waited for me to get home for work, to accuse me of cheating on his mom, that night with a girl he had a crush on, at the job, I got for him. It wasn't about his mom at all, it was about his selfish ass, as I'm pretty sure he had a crush on her. He insisted that she was there, so I dialed the number to the other job where she was working that night, handed him the phone, and said to ask for her. I will be down the road beating the s*** out of that stop sign. When you realize that you are dead wrong, I expect an apology. He somehow managed to give me an apology but it changed nothing! It was way too much for me to handle. My nickname for him was Oedipus. Wonder why!

Now, let's get to the crazy part!

Right after I ended the relationship, she became besties with the girl who lived right across the foyer from me at the condo I moved into. Oh look, another amazing coincidence, this never happens to me. same old s*** huh. This Kind of crap happens to me so many times that it has to be my fault. It's absolutely ridiculous. She ended up really hurting that person she was using. You know, that friend of mine that lived across from me, that she was all the sudden besties with. She thought they were really friends, and was very hurt when she realized she was being used. Somehow after that, they did remain friends. Again, she is not a bad person.

Everywhere I went she would magically show up. I was convinced you had a crystal ball. Was she Magic? She did have a crystal ball after all, it was called Facebook.

My wonderful idiot friend was tagging us everywhere we went. Hey, hey, he is my idiot friend. I'm the only one allowed to call him that! I told him what she was doing and he, in disbelief, said, yeah right. Of course, she just so happened to show up wherever I was why would I think anything else.

All right, tough guy I said, tag us in the bar down the road instead of where we are and I will prove it.

About an hour later we went to the place where he tagged us, and I confronted the bartender, who knew her, and sure enough she was there, looking everywhere, like a lioness that lost her cub. He said she appeared as if she was on a mission. I eventually learned how to use Facebook, to avoid the situation. I would just tag us someplace where we were not, every time, and every time I proved my point.

Another wonderful thing is that she tried to do and succeeded a few times at, was fornicating with my friends and even coworkers. Yep, fucked up!!! I'm choosing not to elaborate on this one.

Okay this one's a little creepy. One of my friends/coworkers went to the condo where she had befriended that poor girl so she could spy on me. He told me he saw her, at 1:30 in the morning, sitting alone in the dark while her new bestie had already gone to sleep. Whatever was she doing sitting alone in the dark at 1:30 in the morning you ask? She was sitting there staring at the front door of a condo where I was staying. EXTRA SPECIAL SUPER CREEPY!!!!.

I do have to say that this person is a good person, and has all her s*** together, however when the heart is involved sometimes decision making goes out the window. She definitely had a temporary absence of sanity!

I almost forgot, she showed up at a friend's birthday karaoke party, and belted out Alanis Morissette's, Jagged Little Pill, and I must say she did a very good job oh, and it worked. I ended up going home with her. You see this is what I've been saying all along. It's not all them, it's very much me, and I understand that.

Last thing. No, really!! She crashed a work Christmas party with one of my friends as her date. I was livid with him, not because it looked like he was going to sleep with my ex. Because he should have known better, and it wrecked the Christmas party for me. How did I know, they weren't going to have sex? Well, he was one of my gay friends, so………. I got over it. He and I are still friends. She did manage to make out with someone, after I left, in a place where everyone could see. That nice man became a very good friend of mine.

Something I should add to this one so that I am being honest. Even though this sounds bad, it wasn't. There is

DEFINITELY another side to this one. This book is about insane stuff. The good stuff GREATLY outweighed the bad, and I would do it all over again. Besides this is just my perspective, and I did plenty of crazy things too. My second book will illustrate that!!!

Chapter 10: The Misdiagnosis

    This one still pisses me off! The main problem here is there's no apology, not even a fake one. All she had to do was say she was sorry and I would have stayed.

    Before I even begin this chapter, she was wrong, the doctor was wrong, and I was closer to correct than all of them. NO exaggeration what so EVER!!!!!!!!!!

    It all started with her having pain during sex and eventually a discharge. The nurses or doctor I can't for the life of me remember who told her it was a PID, which is short for pelvic inflammatory disease. This can only be caused by contracting chlamydia or gonorrhea. She hadn't had sex with anyone for two years, before me. She made the assumption that their diagnosis was correct, even though I told her over and over that it was not. I explained to her that it was probably something much worse if she needed to go back immediately! I kept saying, I have been tested, quite a few times, you are making what could be a life-threatening mistake!!! You need to listen to me.

    Basically, what I'm saying here is she thought I gave her an STD. Are you f****** kidding me? I DID NOT!!!!!   Yep, I'm getting freaking mad again! All she had to do was listen to me and she would have been way better off, she would have been in a lot less pain, and we may even have stayed together, but of course she thought the doctor was right or the nurse or whoever. Jerk offs!!! Being a doctor doesn't automatically mean that person is more intelligent, however it does mean that that person has more drive. A lot of them are very smart, but definitely NOT all of them!!!

    I eventually talked her into going back in to get checked again, and she had a really hard time because of her insurance situation.

    After a month or so went by, she finally got an appointment. The doctor checked her, and with this look of awe and disbelief said, "Who told you that?" Me, knowing all the time, I didn't have an STD, and that I didn't give her an STD said, "Excuse me, I'm sorry but are you saying it was an existing condition?" The doctor said yes!

She had a prolapsed fibroid uterine tumor. He also mentioned that had it not been discovered it might have been a big problem, so basically, I did her a freaking favor. The tumor was prolapsed out of her cervix and during sex, it was being irritated and that was what identified a much larger problem. Had that not happened, it could have grown to the point where it could cause some serious problems. So, not only did I not give her a goddamn thing, I saved her from a lot of pain and suffering! Yep, still pissed, no apology, no nothing. She gave me the cold shoulder for a month because she believed something that wasn't true. It's not like I told her over and over and over and over that the doctor was wrong. I hate this fallacy that everyone thinks that anyone that works in a hospital is always going to be right.

I had to apologize to the doctor for doing a very immature, very in your face, TOLD YOU SO dance. Why did I do that dance? Because I was f****** right!!!

I even said, very sarcastically, "So, this is an existing condition, and because I hit that spot and caused pain and drew attention to the problem, correct? So, in effect, it could have grown to become a serious problem?" He said, "Well yes."

Why the f*** did this girl never give me an apology? I even tried again to ask her for one, years later, and her response was that she didn't diagnose herself with that, the nurse did or the doctor did, or whatever the f*** happened. How about a nice big f*** her for that. I get it, she was going through something, but WTF!!!!

I should add, I'm very glad that she is safe, I'm glad she got it removed, and I'm glad that it's over for her. Again, all she had to do is apologize!

I was very angry, yet relieved, so I repeated myself a few times to make a point. Again, I said, "So, I did not give her an STD, in fact, I found a problem that is a tumor coming out of her cervix, yeah pretty much!" JUST WANTED TO BE CLEAR!!!!!

So effectively this girl treated me like s*** for over a month, realized she was wrong, and never apologized. Well f*** you!!!!!

To this day I am dumbfounded why she wouldn't listen to me. Had I not finally gotten through to her she might have been in serious trouble. No thank you no apology no nothing

Bytches Be Crazy

And yes, I am aware she was going through something pretty intense, but it doesn't mean she gets the right to be shitty to me.

I Thought I was going to try to be friends with this one, but after writing this I don't think I ever want to see her or talk to her again. I did at least stick around, until I knew she was OK.

Kevin Allen

Chapter 11: The Raging Alcoholic

I liked this person quite a bit, but it was made very clear to me right away, that she needed to do a lot of personal healing before she was able to date anyone. She had repeatedly flirted with me at work and of course I flirted back. She was very attractive. I did, at first, think it was all a joke.

How we initially bonded was on me. She came to work one day and she was inconsolable. She was absolutely miserable, and looked like she wanted to die. I decided I was going to make her smile. I said, is it really that bad? She said, there is nothing you can do to make me smile.

I, of course did not accept that answer. So, my response was, well did you shit your pants! She got out of her funk for a second and looked at me discombobulated and confused and said, "Excuse me?"

I said, "Well did you, did you shit your pants?" She started laughing hysterically and said, "No, of course not!"

I said, "Well then it's not really that bad now is it." We became fast friends

She had an awful lot going on which I am not going to mention in this book because even though there are no names in here, I'm just not going to do it. Her situation was awful. I tried to help her by being there as much as I could but it was going to take me down. You can't be there for somebody if you let them take you down. She wasn't trying to, but she would have.

All that being said, this is the crazy part. I decided to come over to her house for a date, sort of, and make drinks for the two of us. I had bought a 1.75 L bottle of decent vodka so that I could leave her some, after we were done. I made us two drinks a piece. She then asked me if I would like to put a movie in to relax and suggested I could pick the movie. This being one of my favorite things to do I immediately left the room to go look through her movie selection.

Kevin Allen

When I returned the whole 1.75 L bottle was gone, and she was sitting in the corner unable to speak or move. I didn't know what to do oh, but I wasn't going to leave her alone. I carried her to her bed and sat with her all night to make sure she was okay. She woke up and she couldn't even open her hands because she was so dehydrated. I got her some Gatorade. She wanted me to get her more vodka. OH, HELLLLLL NO! I said please at least hydrate before you drink anything else. I waited till she seemed to be okay and left. I tried to be there for her a few more times but the situation didn't change. It sucks cuz she was really a great girl oh, but I just can't.

Chapter 12: The Martyr and Her Evil Mother

This person, not the mom, is very sweet, and has been through her own, very rough trials with relationships, and life as well. Although some of her actions are fitting for this book, I can say none of it was done with malice. Her intentions were always good I believe.

That being said, it was still an insane situation the story is going to be told.

The relationship started innocently enough. We were friends, always trying to be there for each other, mostly because we recognize the pain of experiencing a hurtful relationship that causes trauma in the other.

For me, it may have been being chased around my house with my own samurai sword. For her it was a disgusting man that sold drugs and cheated on her every chance he got.

It worked for a while, until it didn't. We decided to live together. The kids were there too. They were work at first having been through a lot too, but I did what I had to do and cared for them.

The PROBLEM was, she moved her mother in who is an ex-heroin/meth addict. Did I say, EX addict? Na, she just traded for morphine and Adderall. WELL SHIT!!! I would like to get off this ride now please!!! Stop the car, I feel sick!!! Am I in another dimension here?

This woman, doctor shops, causes fights, did drugs with her grandson, and was quite the bane of the family.

Yeah, it's a big problem when you have an old lady sitting in the f****** dark with her 15-year-old grandson with his 15-year-old friend! She was definitely the problem! What in the piece of fuck is wrong with her.

I tried to talk to her. I tried to talk to my girl. I tried to talk to her son. No one listened to me.

When I finally left, I was told by everyone that I just ghosted her family. It's not like I tried to talk to her, almost EVERY FRIGGIN DAY!!!! Are you SERIOUS? I tried to talk to her for

MONTHS!!!! Every time I tried to talk to her, she said she'd had too much on her plate, and couldn't handle it right now. I ghosted her, MY ASS!!

We even had a vacation planned that SHE, not I, suggested we get insurance for, in case it didn't work out between us. How the f*** did I ghost her if it was already discussed in length. This is how she played the martyr. I didn't even try to defend myself on this one. I even lost a mutual friend over it.

Let me put it in a nutshell why I left. You moved your druggie mom in with you and your kids. You may have meant well but you were so afraid someone may not like you for it, you never kicked her out. This is your problem not mine.

She actually finally did kick her out after I left. Good for her. I hope your family is well. I'm guessing that they are with the absence of her abusive mother. They are after all good people, just put in a bad situation. It's not like I haven't made plenty of my own bad decisions.

Her mother did drugs with her brother, and her brother ended up in prison. I wasn't about to watch her do that to her grandson. I did everything I could until I lost the ability to show any kindness whatsoever. I was at my limit. I was no longer able to help.

She of course, demonized me, as they all do, even going so far as saying I was on heroin. That is the most ridiculous thing I've ever heard. I'm in my late 40s at the time, with near perfect teeth and I'm in better shape than most 20-year-olds. If you're going to tell a lie, make it believable, you dumbass! Heroin, are you f****** kidding me. Just another wow moment in my dating career. F****** good luck selling that one!!! She did at least do me a favor slinging that monkey feces. After that no one believed a f****** word out of her mouth, well, about me anyways.

Of course, she was an angel that never did anything wrong to anyone ever, wah wah wah, no one is ever fair for her she does everything for everybody. I HATE MARTYRS!!!!!! They are such perfect little angels in their stories aren't they.

Just a little flavor I'd like to add at the end to leave ya, thinking WTF:

A few of her coworkers approached me and told me that she had a calendar where she had marked down each time I decided to go out with friends for drinks. It turns out it was about, once a month. She eventually showed me the calendar, but I swore that I wouldn't tell her that I already knew about it. UM, that's a little crazy! No, that's a lot crazy!

She had tallied up about 5 months before even showing me. That is some premeditated s*** right there!

She had the nerve to chastise me for going out, ONCE A MONTH. I don't think that's a problem, in fact I think that was perfectly healthy.

I remember saying, hold on, you are really upset with me for going out once a month. I have to deal with an indescribable amount of bullshit, every day, like your family doing drugs in the house, the s*** I had to do with your kids at first, your drug addicted mom causing problems, you getting mad at me for wanting to buy a specific f****** car for myself. f*** you!!!!!!!!!! I really wanted that car. I still don't understand that.

I should get a f****** trophy for only going out once a month. The f*** is wrong with you!!! What kind of f***** up control issues was that. Holy Shit, I sure can pick them can't I

Kevin Allen

Chapter 13: The Bathtub

Some of these stories are more insane than others. This one is pretty tame by comparison, and that being said, pretty short. The reason it made it into the book was because I was put in harm's way due to decisions based purely on emotion, which is a deal-breaker! 100% goodbye, kind of stuff. I will never understand such behavior, nor will I EVER behave in such a manner.

The relationship was pretty nice until the honeymoon phase was over. In this person's defense she was dealing with ovarian cysts. When they would burst it would hurt her so bad, she would fall to the ground and I would pick her up and carry her wherever she needed to go. Most common treatment for this is to administer estrogen, which is most commonly done in the form of a birth control pill. In an unfair outcome for her, it caused her to become severely off-kilter. It wasn't her fault.

I'm about to describe the only nutbar situation she put me in, however, it is UNFORGIVABLE. I do not care how emotional someone gets; they should NEVER put someone else in harm's way. This has happened to me more than once and no amount of apologies will ever fix it. it is something that I would never ever ever ever ever ever ever ever ever do!!!!

We were in the bathroom at a party at our house having a private conversation that stemmed from a disagreement. All of a sudden started flipping out and tried to barrel through me to get to the door. It was completely unnecessary; I have no intentions of blocking it. I do understand, she may have felt trapped. It was not my intention. It was her suggestion to use the bathroom to have a private conversation. The bathroom is small, in an attempt to get out of her way a very gently bumped her, accidentally and hardly at all.

I then watched her look at the tub and then throw herself in it as if I had pushed her. It was amazing how she landed perfectly in the tub, without injuring herself whatsoever, almost as if it was premeditated. Hmmmmmm. She was standing perpendicular to the tub and then somehow managed, while airborne, to end up parallel to it and land ever so gently. What kind of b******* is that. yep, here we go again!

That's not even the part that's unforgivable. What comes next is! She lets out a scream, and then yells he's beating me! What in the holy fuck, are you kidding me? I can't believe I'm going through this kind of s*** again. I have got to stop putting myself in situations with people that will put me in f****** danger just because they're having an emotional outburst!! Again, that s*** is UNFORGIVEABLE!!!

Here is a nice little variable that will aid is describing the brevity of the situation. Most of the guys at that party were bodybuilders and thank God they all knew who I was, and that I was incapable of such a thing, so they all brushed off the accusation completely.

I of course left, and as she tried to convince me to stay, I explained that trying to put me in harm's way, even if it was in a heightened emotional state magnified by orally induced estrogen is a NO GO!

IT IS AN ABSOLUTE DEAL BREAKER!!!!! I knew that if something bad happened stemming from her asinine outburst, that she would immediately change her tune and step in because she was wrong and I knew she didn't want to actually hurt me, however this is just something you do not ever ever do!!! Not sure why, but it seems that this is only done by people that "care" about me.

Chapter 14: The Convenient Friend

    This isn't really about one person this time, it's about most of the situations I've been in. How is it that after I exit a situation for my own health, the person I walk away from magically becomes besties with one of my friends, family members, a roommate, people I work with, or anyone around me. WTF!!!

    No consideration whatsoever for the person that is being pulled into a fake friendship for purely selfish reasons

    I have had several of my friends fall for this really get hurt when they find out that they were just being used all the time. On the other hand, sometimes, our friendship blossoms out of it, but not without hurt feelings first

    If you ever do this to someone, YOU MY FRIEND, ARE A SOCIOPATH!!!

    I always try to warn my friends and they always reply with the same thing. It's not about you, she's my friend. It's not like I haven't earned my degree in crazy shit or anything. What do I know? How conceited of me! Sigh! Then they find out I was trying to help them and not only are they hurt, but they feel stupid for not listening to me. I understand that people make bad decisions when they're hurt, but people are not to become collateral damage, for some stupid immature agenda! Please stop doing this. Being inconsiderate even if accidental, is still just that, inconsiderate!

Chapter 15: Stockholm Syndrome

Writing this chapter is very sad for me and it's going to bring a few tears. This poor woman was in a terrible situation and it hurt me tremendously to walk away but I had to. I was not going to survive it.

It made me dangerously reckless and I moved 1300 miles away to save myself from it.

To this day I beat myself up for maybe not trying harder.

This chapter is unique because the craziness was clearly from another source, and was so powerful and manipulative it translated to her.

I met this person through working for her father, who was a man I respected and worked very hard for. He wasn't without his faults, no more than I am without mine. I believe he wanted me to save his daughter from that awful person. Normally, I would not try to involve myself with someone who was taken, but this man is pure evil, the likes of which I've never seen before.

Her relationship with her awful boyfriend was so bad, the father wanted me to save her from him, at least that's how I interpreted it. I loved her dad and was elated for a chance to be part of that family. I loved each of her siblings for different reasons, and her mother was an angel, and I mean, an ANGEL!

So, she and I finally found a way to sneak away for a little vacation after a year of talking about what ifs. It was pure Heaven.

When we were there, I made every meal for her except for when we went out to eat. I spoiled her for sure. I wanted her to know what being treated right was like. She didn't even know how to deal with it. She kept saying, "Wow, is this my life now?" I was so happy; I'm actually crying a little writing this.

When we got home from our lovely little sabbatical from the ugliness of life, she got up the nerve to call that piece of s***, and say it's over I'm with a better man now.

Next thing you know there are pictures popping up on her cell phone of that jackass holding a gas can over her dog and her clothes with the text, I'll burn your house down and kill your dog. She immediately left. I couldn't bear it for very long and that was pretty much the end of it, as sad as it was. Did I mention that a house she had before, mysteriously burned down. INTERESTING!!!! HMMMM. However, could that have happened? This guy is the ultimate piece of s***!

Let's do an inventory of some of the things that I knew with this freaking guy did. This guy punched her sweet little brother, pulled a knife on a couple or family members, including her mother, cheated on her, stole from her, and is drinking himself to death, you name it he's done it. As far as I'm concerned, he's the biggest piece of s*** to walk the earth. He is exactly the opposite of what I spent my life striving to be.

One time he even tried to fight me, and I just embarrassed himself. And no, I didn't hurt him, it would have just made things exponentially worse for her. That kind of thing NEVER works!

I was honestly prepared to devote my life to making her happy, but in the end, I ran away because I couldn't bear the pain. I hate this chapter.

Chapter 16: The Stripper

    I met a beautiful Japanese woman in California. SHE suggested I ask her for an engagement. I did. We were engaged, I think. Did it on a lifeguard station on the beach. She had 2 kids. They were great. She one day asked if she could work as a stripper. I informed her that it was not my decision, however if it changed her, as I feared it would, I would leave. It did. I left! The end.

Kevin Allen

Chapter 17: The Three-Month Marriage

Let's just say, I was drinking a lot back then. Yes, let's say that. I remember her saying, you're going to marry me, at least once a day. I ended up doing all the legwork, paid all the fees and the stuff, then called her and said okay, let's get married. I must have been out of my mind.

The marriage may have been a sham but the wedding was gorgeous. We all wore light blue tops and white pants and did it on the beach. It was really nice. When did it all go south you ask? As soon as I signed the marriage certificate, that's when! Holy s***!!! Her head spun all the way around and she puked projectile green split pea looking soup that was made by a syphilitic demon. I was sure we were going to need an exorcism! My best man looked at me as if to say dude you're f*****. He said all that was just a glance.

There wasn't much to recall, except for the constant nastiness. We were both working about 40 or so hours a week then all the sudden I was up to 70 and she was down to 20. I would get yelled at as soon as I walked in the house and did all the cooking and most of the cleaning as well. She argued about everything. Nothing she did was wrong of course.

One of my favorite memories was the turkey bacon incident. She filled the grocery cart with garbage food and then decided that she was going to be healthy by eating turkey bacon. This girl ate McDonald's every day. I of course removed the turkey bacon from the cart and got regular bacon. Turkey bacon is blasphemy!

My favorite thing she said was I can't wait to get pregnant so I don't have to work anymore. WHAT? WHAT? WHAT?

This is NOT, why you bring a child into the world!!! OMG, you have to be kidding me. At the risk of being to descript, I did some things by myself and ensured I had no swimmers left by the time she got home.

She even tried to tell me that reality TV was real. She thought she was going to be on some awful country music reality show. When we got together, I established one rule, watch it all you want just make sure I'm not in the freaking house. She promised not to watch that garbage when I was home. I mean I worked all the time so how hard was that. You all know, she did it anyway.

As fate would have it, she ended up working at a very popular car dealership that wound up having a reality TV show within it. She was often given small parts from time to time. She eventually admitted to me that I was right and it's all scripted. No s*** Sherlock!

Wait a minute I'm sorry what? I was right? Like they would ever risk their money on a chance that it wouldn't be entertaining!

When we got divorced, she attempted to get a restraining order on me with fake makeup bruises. I left court with a permanent felony restraining order on her, which she broke over and over and over.

She would even show up to my job as a liaison from her job to trade out gift cards to increase business. What!

My idiot boss tried to defend it. THIS IS NOT A COINCIDENCE!!! Are you guys seeing a pattern here? Same old s***!

I would like to end this chapter with my very favorite part.

When we finally got divorced some guy had knocked her up and was with her. He was really nice. I heard her say, oh wow this is going by fast I won't have to be late to work. then, to my delight, and also proving me right, he said, hey honey when you're at work if you're not done continuously bitching at everyone could you stay the f*** there!

All I could think was, you poor bastard. I'm getting out but you got her pregnant. That poor nice man. We shared a glance and understood each other. I wonder if she ended up eating him.

Chapter 18: Misery

We got a doozy right here, and I mean WOW! HOLY SHIT!!, WTF?, kind of stuff. How was I so blinded to let all this happen? You might just figure it out when you read this.

My mother referred to this relationship as misery, yes, like the movie, where she broke the guy's freaking leg so he couldn't get away.

I was definitely hobbled, but not like that. It was done chemically and financially. For any people that know me that happen to read this don't worry about it, it's over. Now let's Wander over to the beginning of how this all happened.

I had bought myself a very expensive 150cc scooter. The thing was actually pretty cool, it went 100 mph, had a remote-control starter, alarm system, and all the bells and whistles. I loved it. Yeah, I know oh, it was still a scooter. Shout out to all my biker friends! I still joke about crashing it and my Jesus looking wonderful biker buddy has a good laugh at my expense every time. Not because I crashed, but because I had a scooter. Ahhh, the bromance!

Back to me crashing it. I was banged up pretty bad. I have 10 inches of titanium in my left leg, where the bone was completely shattered and then some metal in my right arm as well.

This crash led me to need some help, and who better to do that than the sweet girl I used to work with, that unbeknownst to me, had decided to make money selling pills. Jesus, I can pick em! GREAT!!!! I didn't ignore that red flag. That shining bright gigantic red flag. I didn't even know it was there!

I gave her access to my bank account and agreed to financially help her if she helped me. I asked her to please administer these awful pain meds I was given, as when I took them, I had no concept of time whatsoever. They were very powerful. It was either that or be in excruciating pain. In hindsight, having the knowledge I have now I would have opted for the pain. I instructed her to make sure I had no more than 2 a day because they were so very strong. I was quite literally out of my mind.

Without my knowledge she had been using my money to purchase more pills, and kept feeding them to me, hence the hobbling. By the time I figured it out I was physically addicted, and had to get a hotel room for a week with liquid vitamin B, honey, a huge water cooler, and several bottles of bubble gum vodka to try it at least get some kind of sleep. Was able to successfully get off of those horrible things. I told my doctor about how I did it and he was amazed. He told me that most people could not do such a thing, and many had taken their own lives doing so. My response was to show him the molecular structure of the pills, right next to the molecular structure of heroin. Oddly, he could not tell the difference. I exhibited my disgust. Big Pharma is criminal!

It was absolute horror, and I mean HORROR!!!! There were a few times I thought that maybe I died when I crashed the scooter and this was hell. No exaggeration! Whomever made these things is a monster. What made me take notice of the problem was one day when I was looking for my driver's license. I found an old one and I found a more recent one. The difference in my physical appearance over the time that I had taken those awful things was something I was not willing to accept. OMG!!! NOPE! NOPE! NOPE!!!

I had become physically weak as well. I remember my Mom calling me telling me that she just did 30 push-ups. I, of course, was impressed with her. My mom thought she was Rocky, and she kind of was. Curious, I tried, and only got 6. HELLLLL NO!!!!! I had done over a hundred before. This was not happening. I do not see myself as a weak person, nor will I allow it to ever happen.

I started pretending to take those awful pills, as she handed them to me, and cupped them in my hand instead of ingesting them, then threw them away. I can still hear her voice. You want medicine in that sweet little sick, demon voice. This was the worst kind of manipulation I've ever experienced and had no f****** idea it was going on. I thought she was helping me. Now recalling the memory of that voice makes me want to puke. I almost did just writing this now.

I went from having over $100,000 in the bank to living in her sister's basement in Ohio. I tried to help her sister around the house, so I didn't feel like a piece of s***. She forbade it. I tried to get a job. She forbade it. She was making it so I couldn't possibly get away. My leg was still healing, my arm was still healing and she kept all the money away from me. I kept asking myself how I allowed this to happen. The answer is, I don't know.

I did find a way to survive financially. I would get broken, or really cheap computers off of Craigslist and fix them up and sell them to make some money. She would always handle the money and leave me with just enough money to survive, and not enough money to get out of that freaking hell.

This person's mood swings were astronomical which is another thing that drew my attention to what was going on. She was always chewing on a straw, which was odd, but whatever. I didn't realize it was the biggest red flag on the planet!!!!

One of my friends advised me to watch her closely and to be careful not to allow her to see me watching.

I employed the use of a mirror at a restaurant to observe. I saw things I had no idea I was going to see.   What in God's name have I gotten myself into. This was unreal. I saw her put 3, yes three kinds of pills in a straw, and chew it, crushing all 3 into a powder, then flipped it over and quickly snorted them all at once when she felt no one was looking. Holy s***, holy s***, holy s***. Upon further researching it turned out that there was an oxycodone, an Adderall, and a Klotopin. How is she alive you asked oh, she's not anymore. It eventually killed her a few years later after I was away from her.

Escape is a pretty strong word I realize, but that's how I feel. I managed to hide enough money over time to hopefully get a bus ticket back to Florida.

I wasn't really ready to go yet, but that's not usually how it works out is it? We got in some stupid argument, and she made the mistake of saying something about my late fiancé. I said to myself, you know what, she is watching. I am the f*** out of here!

I rode a bike, mind you, with a broken arm and a broken leg for at least 7 miles to get to a bus station. I barely had enough to get home, so the nice woman at the desk gave me a military discount.

I told her she should keep the bike I rode and gave her the key to the lock because I wasn't taking it with me. I was finally free! I left everything! I left two cars, two bikes, furniture, name it! All I took was a backpack. I met that girl on the bus that I spoke of in the prelude on that trip home.

Jeez!!!!

AND, You guessed it, it's not over. That THING followed me back to Florida and would return my belongings to me, one at a time, so I was forced to see her. The last time I saw her she got pulled over and the police officer started a purse looking for drugs. He found them.

I was absolutely mortified. I rolled down the window and explained to the officer that I was just trying to get my belongings back. I just wanted to get away from her forever. The officer kindly suggested I run while I can. I did!

One of my very best friends who lived across the country got wind of the whole ordeal and flew me to Virginia to stay with him, to make sure I was free of her. I ended up helping raise his 2-year-old little girl for a spell and got to see him meet the love of his life, and I mean soulmate! I never saw anything like it.

PHEW!!!, It's over!! NOPE, just kidding!!! She had bought herself a lot of furniture and entertainment things with my money. I had a friend with a family that had nothing and I really wanted to help.

I called and called and called, trying to get it back for this friend. It was painful. I did not want to talk to her. I remember that I felt so bad about it I even called my mother and asked if I was doing the right thing. My mother was the sweetest person alive. She said screw her, get it back. My friend I was trying to help saw how hard it was for me and didn't want me to do it. I decided to try one more thing before I gave up.

I called her mother. I told her I needed that back to set up an apartment for us, and surprise her. She mailed me a key to the storage unit oh, I got all my stuff back oh, and I gave it to my friend. I was able to take something shitty and turn it into something wonderful. O.K., it's really over this time.

Chapter 19: Narcissist Supreme

I'm not sure which one was the worst, this one or the last one. It's pretty close but this one got to my family.

I had never seen such an insane level of insecurity. I couldn't even order a drink from a female bartender without getting attacked as soon as I got home about it. Mind you, I'm a very friendly person and talk to everybody. I would talk to all kinds of people and it was never a problem until it was a female. It was all the same to me. I just like to talk to people.

Most of the stories I tried to be a little nice maybe even provide some kind of reason for erratic behavior but NOT THIS ONE!!!

This one infiltrated my family and caused me more problems than you can imagine, and I am someone that has been given up to a foster home during puberty and was taken back, thank GOD. It seemed to reason; I already had some family issues. All Is Forgiven by the way, and I love my family. That POS only cared about herself. I didn't even know what narcissist meant before her. She is The Narcissist Supreme!

Of course, the universe sent me a red flag. We had dated before when we were young. She hurt me really bad. It was like she was trying to get myself in her ex-boyfriend to fight over her. She ended up going back to him. Even after they broke up, she reported everything to his family she could to destroy him. He eventually took his own life. Is it related, who knows, but after she did the same thing to me, I have to say probably yes. That piece of garbage even warned me that if I did not come back to her, I would regret it. So, her getting what she wanted was more important than my relationship with my family. Yeah, she SUCKED!!!

I remember going out for a few drinks with her. I'm a very outgoing person. I'll talk to anybody. It was always okay until it was a female other than a little old lady. I couldn't even order a drink from a female bartender without her quietly waiting till we got home and then viciously verbally attacking me. I didn't understand. I never cheated on her and never intended to.

She kept saying I was putting myself out there. She never actually said it but I was not allowed to speak to another woman. It was insane. She would follow me around the house screaming at me until I would finally yell back and then suddenly, I was the bad guy for yelling as she so eloquently martyred herself.

She had the same story for every relationship, how she was a perfect angel and did everything for them, and they just walked away.

She made this one-man sound so bad I went to the bar he worked at and I picked his brain. Turns out he had similar stories to mine. He was actually afraid to say anything about her. It was obvious, I was fucked

She always said she didn't think it was fair that his family wouldn't talk to her as they were married previously. I wish my family would have done the same. She wreaked havoc on mine, and tried to do the same with his. Rewind to the guy that took his own life, yeah, his family stayed in touch with her.

I didn't know if it was a disorder or she was just evil, but there is no excuse for that. There is never a reason to estrange a man's mother from him. She is an absolute piece of s***.

When I left her, she went to my very best friend's house every day and complained about me until he finally threw her out.

After that she went to my younger sister's house. This went on until my family decided to have a freaking intervention for me. My poor Dad was just trying to help, as she is quite the actress. I don't blame my family for this. She had me believing the same s*** about her ex.

I warned my father that if this is what I thought it was it wasn't going to go as planned.

Oh, and it was! My stupid ass told her that the only way my ex before her, also known as the Revenge Fornicator was able to hurt me was through my family. I even told her what she said. All she had to do was repeat the information. Now my family has heard it from two sources. This made it real in their mind. They just wanted to help. 100% backfire!!! To get away from the situation, I walked about 15 mi in the snow, by my damn self in a freaking t-shirt. I told them they would never see me again! I see them all the time now, and they are wonderful. I am very fortunate to have them. This was just how I felt at the time.

I'm going to end this with something good that came from this nightmare. She and I are on a Valentine's date. We went to see Deadpool at the movies. She was on her phone texting the whole time, most likely to one of the two guys she spoke to every day, before bed, and first thing in the morning. Remember I was not allowed to so much as speak to another woman. We went to dinner afterward. She was still on her phone.

I had enough! Rules for me, NONE FOR HER!!!! There was always some dire reason why it was okay for her to do whatever she wanted, and I just had to deal with it.

I would like to end this with something good that spawned from this evil.

I spot this lovely couple at the bar, and I say excuse me, I know it's Valentine's Day and you too are ridiculously adorable, but would you like to take a funny wager? Loser buys a drink. Sure, they both said Okay, see that girl on the phone over there? Well, that's my date. I'm willing to bet it'll be 20 minutes before she looks up and sees that I am not sitting there. What's your bet? Closest to it wins. I won, almost exactly the time it took. The couple are still very good friends and I cherish that friendship. They are truly wonderful people.

She still haunts me though. I had the opportunity to work with an amazing Chef who I have the utmost respect for. I found out she used to work there and was always afraid she would get to him and taint our relationship. This is just one example. I get nervous every time I am around anyone that knows her. I get a little nauseous even.

Thank God I haven't heard from her in years.

Sum it all up:

Most of the people I have spoken of in this book are very good people that were put in situations where they behaved poorly. All of us have behaved poorly when matters of the heart are involved, myself included, probably more so than others.

There are a few, however, that are just really bad people and I have no apologies.

I hope this was entertaining for you. Some of it was hard to write. Some of it was funny. Some of it even made me sick. All in all, It definitely helped me to realize my part in it all. There are always two sides to each story. This is just my side of the story. Look out for book 2, featuring their side of the story, and book 3, which is full of guest stories. I have instructed them to show no mercy. This is going to hurt.

Kevin Allen

Bytches Be Crazy

Starry Night Publishing

Everyone has a story...

Don't spend your life trying to get published! Don't tolerate rejection! Don't do all the work and allow the publishing companies to reap the rewards!

Millions of independent authors like you are making money, publishing their stories now. Our technological know-how will take the headaches out of getting published. Let Starry Night Publishing take care of the hard parts, so you can focus on writing. You simply send us your Word Document, and we do the rest. It really is that simple!

The big companies want to publish only "celebrity authors," not the average book-writer. It is almost impossible for first-time authors to get published today. This has led many authors to go the self-publishing route. Until recently, this was considered "vanity-publishing." You spent large sums of your money to get twenty copies of your book, to give to relatives at Christmas just so you could see your name on the cover. However, the self-publishing industry allows authors to get published in a timely fashion, retain the rights to your work, keeping up to ninety percent of your royalties instead of the traditional five percent.

We have opened the gates, allowing you inside the world of publishing. While others charge you as much as fifteen-thousand dollars for a publishing package, we charge less than five-hundred dollars to cover copyright, ISBN, and distribution costs. Do you really want to spend all your time formatting, converting, designing a cover, and then promoting your book because no one else will?

Our editors are professionals, able to create a top-notch book that you will be proud of. Becoming a published author is supposed to be fun, not a hassle.

Kevin Allen

At Starry Night Publishing, you submit your work, we create a professional-looking cover, a table of contents, compile your text and images into the appropriate format, convert your files for eReaders, take care of copyright information, assign an ISBN, allow you to keep one-hundred-percent of your rights, distribute your story worldwide on Amazon, Barnes and Noble and many other retailers, and write you a check for your royalties. There are no other hidden fees involved! You do not pay extra for a cover or to keep your book in print. We promise! Everything is included! You even get a free copy of your book and unlimited half-price copies.

In twelve short years, we have published more than six thousand books, compared to the major publishing houses, which only add an average of six new titles per year. We will publish your fiction or non-fiction books about anything and look forward to reading your stories and sharing them with the world.

We do all subject matter, fiction, or nonfiction, scholarly works, cookbooks, self-help, etc. Our company might not be huge in size, but we currently have more than 6,500 clients, maintain an A+ rating with the Better Business Bureau, of which we are an accredited member, and have won the "Best of Rochester" Business Award four years in a row, making us a member of the Rochester Business Hall of Fame.

We sincerely hope that you will join the growing Starry Night Publishing family, become a published author, and gain the world-wide exposure that you deserve. You deserve to succeed. Success comes to those who make opportunities happen, not those who wait for opportunities to happen. You just have to try. Thanks for joining us on our journey.

www.starrynightpublishing.com

www.facebook.com/starrynightpublishing/

Made in the USA
Coppell, TX
01 September 2023